The Life and Times of

Joseph E. Clark

From Slavery to Town Father
(Eatonville, Florida)

Pen & Ink drawing of Joseph E. Clark (circa 1910)
Barbara Winsor, Artist

The Life and Times of
Joseph E. Clark

From Slavery to Town Father
(Eatonville, Florida)

by
Olga Fenton Mitchell
and
Gloria Fenton Magbie

with

Marion Civette Elden

Four-G Publishers, Inc.

2003

Mitchell, Olga Fenton
    The Life and Times of Joseph E. Clark—From Slavery to Town Father, by Olga Fenton Mitchell and Gloria Fenton Magbie, with Marion Civette Elden.
    112 pages, 28 cm.
    ISBN: 1885066-341

For copies of the book and inquiries, contact:
Olga Fenton Mitchell
P. O. Box 771503
Orlando, FL 32877-1503
E-mail: joeclark50@aol.com

Price: $12.95
Add: $2.25, taxes, shipping, & handling

Published by
FOUR-G Publishers, Inc.
P. O. Box 1575, Jonesboro, AR 72401
TEL: 870-934-0418

Cover Design by
Marion Civette Elden, Editor, *Life at Hunter's Creek*
with
Mary Wismar-Davis, Editor, *Rollins College Alumni Record*

Replication of Original Painting of Early Eatonville
Courtesy of Louise Franklin

TABLE OF CONTENTS

The Life and Times of Joseph E. Clark
From Slavery to Town Father

1880 - 1899 - FLORIDA

BOOK IV — 1900 - 1911 - SUCCESS

BOOK V — THE PRESENT

This Book is

Dedicated

to the

Loving Memory

of our

Mother — Bertha Pryor Fenton

and

Grandmother — Mattie Clark Pryor Dennis

Mattie Clark Pryor Dennis,
oldest daughter of
Joseph E. Clark
(circa 1930)

Bertha Mae Pryor Fenton,
granddaughter of
Joseph E. Clark
(circa 1962)

Introduction I

When we retired in 1996, Mitch and I moved to Orlando, Florida from Greenwood Lake, New York. The following year, while reading the *Orlando Sentinel* I saw a picture of Joe Clark in an article about Eatonville. For years our grandmother had constantly talked to my sister Gloria and me about our great-grandfather, Joe Clark, and what a "big man" he was. We always thought it was just "grandma talking" and "big" meant stature. Suddenly I realized "big" meant important, and the Joe Clark in the picture was our great-grandfather. Thus, the picture was the catalyst that propelled me into researching our family history and culminated in the writing of this book. Although the research was very time-consuming and intensive, it also proved very gratifying and educational.

My sister, Gloria, and I share with you what we've learned about our family from 1859 to 1911, from slavery to freedom, from the past to the present. This book is very close to our hearts. We hope that you enjoy it.

Olga Fenton Mitchell

Introduction II

Olga, Mitch, my husband Ray, and I have been dear friends and neighbors since we moved to Orlando, Florida from Massachusetts. After Olga's propitious reading of an *Orlando Sentinel* article about Eatonville, she embarked on an extensive search to ascertain her ancestry, leading her to discover that the founder of Eatonville was her great-grandfather, Joseph E. Clark.

When she approached me about collaborating with her to write a book about her family, I couldn't refuse. Her enthusiasm was so contagious that "No" was not a word I could have used. As I read Olga's notes, pored over her all-encompassing research, and consulted textbooks pertaining to the life and times of her great-grandfather Joseph E. Clark, I became enlightened and very involved. I gained knowledge of her ancestors; of slavery and the determination it took to rise above it; to become more than is expected of you.

This is to thank you publicly, Olga, for allowing me to be a part of your "Labor of Love." It has also become my "Labor of Love."

Marion Civette Elden

Acknowledgments

Our sincere appreciation to the following people for their invaluable support and aid:

Irene Logan, Historian, Maitland Historical Society and Museums, Florida
. . . for being the source of many historical facts and for being my constant inspiration.

Dannie Helm, Curator, Maitland Historical Society and Museums, Florida
. . . for being so cooperative with my research efforts.

Louise M. Franklin, Historian, Eatonville Historical Preservation Board
. . . for sharing her knowledge and historical papers.

Anthony Knight, Jr., Manager of African American Initiatives, Atlanta History Center, Georgia
. . . for his respect and understanding.

Dr. Tiffany Ruby Patterson, Assoc. Professor, Binghamton University, Binghamton, NY
. . . for her recommendations, guidance, and for being my special "reader."

Alice M. Grant, Orlando, Florida
. . . for her contribution of historical details of Eatonville.

Earnest Smith, Jr., Orlando, Florida
. . . for providing research direction after a providential meeting when my car broke down in Orlando.

Pamela Churchill, wonderful friend
. . . for being so supportive and for visiting many of the archives with me.

And a Special Thanks:
to my husband **Calvin Mitchell**
. . . for supporting and encouraging me and showing me what a true "helpmate" is.

Genealogy Chart — The Joseph E. Clark Family

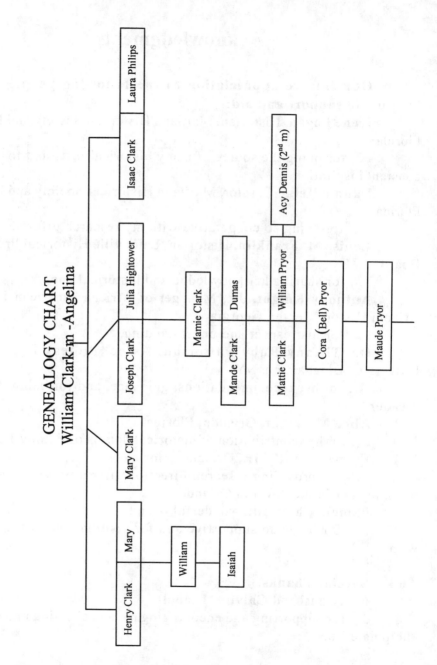

GENEALOGY CHART
William Clark-m -Angelina

Henry Clark — Mary — Mary Clark — Joseph Clark — Julia Hightower — Isaac Clark — Laura Philips

William — Isaiah

Mamie Clark

Mande Clark — Dumas

Mattie Clark — William Pryor — Acy Dennis (2nd m)

Cora (Bell) Pryor

Maude Pryor

Genealogy Chart — The Joseph E. Clark Family

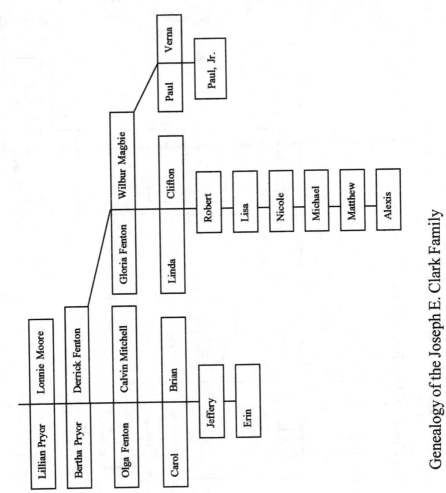

Genealogy of the Joseph E. Clark Family
Compiled by Olga Fenton Mitchell

Genealogy Chart — The Isaac Clark Family

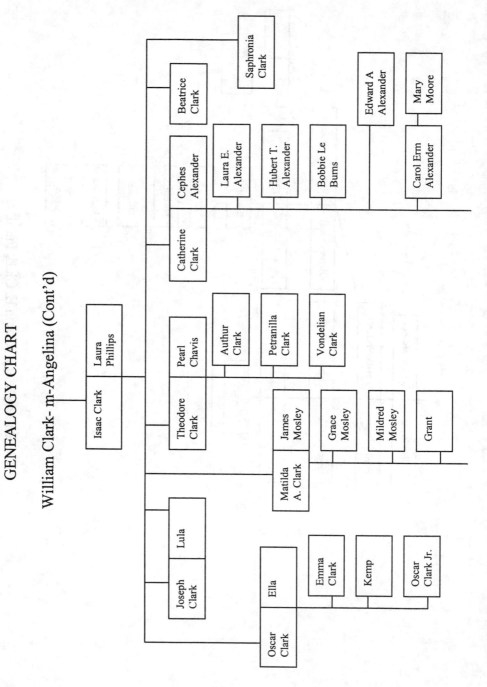

GENEALOGY CHART

William Clark- m-Angelina (Cont'd)

Genealogy Chart — The Isaac Clark Family

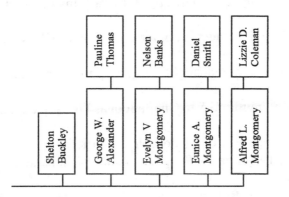

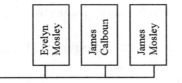

Genealogy of the Isaac Clark Family
Compiled by Angela Montgomery

List of Photographs & Illustrations

Book I

❖   ❖   ❖

1859 - 1865
The Beginning

Chapter 1

SLAVERY AND THE CIVIL WAR

Slavery they can have anywhere. It is a weed that grows in every soil.
Edmund Burke

Joseph Clark was born into slavery—a system that evolved over several centuries. It was a history full of violence which left an indelible mark on him. It impelled him throughout his life to strive to better his circumstances and to exist in a free society . . . his impetus to establish Eatonville.

Africans were sold into slavery and brought over to the "new country," America, to form the backbone of the workers on plantations. As America expanded, and new states applied for admission to the Union, ugly sectional cracks appeared across the facade of nationalism during the tenure of fifth president, James Monroe (1817-1825). Before that time the public paid little attention to the slavery question. Then in February, 1819, the people of the Missouri Territory applied for admission as a slave state and the slavery issue in the United States was dramatically brought to everyone's attention. In the words of elder statesman Thomas Jefferson, people were awakened to the gravity of the issue "as though a fire bell had rung in the night."

Because slavery was already lawful in the territory, it was taken for granted that Missouri would enter the Union as a slave state. However, shortly after the bill of 1819 was presented in the Missouri House of Representatives authorizing Missouri to draw up a constitution for statehood, Representative James Talmadge of New York introduced an amendment to the bill presented to Congress from Missouri. He moved that no more slaves be brought into the new state, and that all children born of slaves in Missouri after the state's admission should be free at the age of 25. Although the representatives from Southern states were alarmed at these proposals, free-state members approved them. The amendment passed by a vote of 87 to 76 after three days of heated debates in the House, but the issue continued to rage throughout the country.

There were many reasons why the struggle over the expansion of slave territory had not begun earlier. Slave states were satisfied with the compromises that had been written into the Constitution on the subject, and importation of slaves was authorized until 1808. Slaves who escaped from a slave state to a free state were required by Congress to be returned. As far west as the Mississippi River, a well-understood boundary line between slave states and free states had been established. East of the state of Ohio, the boundary was the Mason and Dixon Line. From Pennsylvania to the Mississippi River, the boundary was the Ohio River.

Most importantly, a balance had been kept between slave states and free states. There were then 11 of each; and in the United States Senate, the senators from slave and free states were equal in number. This balance of power was especially useful to the South. The Senate rejected the Talmadge Amendment, and Missouri continued to press for admission into the Union. The future boundary between slave states and free states in the Louisiana Purchase territory had to be defined.

After two years of bitter debate in Congress, the Missouri Compromise Bill of 1820 resolved the struggle when Maine sought admission as a free state. Senator Jesse B. Thomas of Illinois proposed that, with the exception of Missouri, new slave states should not be made out of the territory included in the Louisiana Purchase north of 36 degrees, 30" N. Latitude, the contemplated southern boundary of Missouri; thus, pairing Missouri as a slave state with Maine, a free state, and barring slavery north and west of Missouri forever.

In the 1850s, continued westward expansion forced the issue of slavery to the forefront of American politics and Senator Henry Clay introduced the Compromise of 1850, which admitted California as a free state. However, in order to demonstrate the federal government's fundamental support for slavery, a federal Fugitive Slave Law was established and passed by Congress, giving the federal government jurisdiction over runaway slaves. This Fugitive Slave Law was disputed and tested in the famed Dred Scott Decision of 1857. Dred Scott was a black slave who belonged to an officer in the United States Army. His master had taken him from the slave state of Missouri to the free state of Illinois and then to the Wisconsin

5

Territory, which was declared a free territory by the Missouri Compromise of 1820. The officer died in Missouri, after being ordered back there by the Army and taking Scott with him.

Because he had lived on free soil, Scott sued, claiming he was no longer a slave. The case was brought before the United States Supreme Court, and in 1857 a majority of the court (seven out of nine) declared that Scott was still a slave, not a citizen, and had no constitutional right to sue in a federal court. The Dred Scott Decision stated further that Congress had no power to prohibit slavery in the territories and that the Missouri Compromise was unconstitutional. The ruling against Scott pushed the country closer to Civil War.

President James Buchanan urged all Americans to accept the decision of the Supreme Court as final, but antislavery leaders in the North continued their struggle against slavery. The Dred Scott Decision of 1857 convinced many Northerners that Southern slaveholders were determined to rule the nation, which served to widen the gap between the North and South and helped bring on the American Civil War.

The past at least is secure.

Daniel Webster
American statesman
(1782 - 1862)

Chapter 2

JOSEPH CLARK: GENESIS

*People will not look forward to posterity, who
never look backward to their ancestors.*
Edmund Burke

Thrust into this turbulent and unsettling age, in the Year of our Lord 1859, was Joseph. (Cudjo Lewis, was the sole survivor of what is believed to be the last unofficial slave ship to America in 1859.) He was the third child born of black slaves, William and Angelina, on the plantation of N. N. Clark, in Covington, Georgia. His siblings were Henry and Mary. Verifying this is the U. S. Census of 1860 listing Joseph's mother, 30 year-old Angelina; his father William, age 28; brother Henry, 16; sister Mary, three; and Joseph, just one-year old; as black slave inhabitants in the County of Covington, State of Georgia.

There were 54 slaves (22 female and 32 males) on the Clark plantation, and life was very hard. The men worked long hours in the fields. Women also worked in the fields, as well as becoming the support system of breeders and servitude. They were considered assets that could be sold off as they came of age. At that time slaves were given as wedding gifts. The value of girls and women was very low and only the strong survived. Individual slave resistance included mothers killing their newborn babies to save them from slavery, and slaves running away.

Mary, even though she was just going on four years of age, was assigned to look after her younger brother, Joseph. As Joseph grew up, he came to rely more on Mary, who actually raised him, than he did his Mother—who had to put in long hours of labor on the plantation. This closeness of age and the sharing of experiences created an unbreakable and lasting bond, so much so that when Joseph married, his three daughters were given names starting with the letter "M." Mary's premature death in her early teens left Joseph shattered and devastated.

Although Joseph's family lived in slavery, not all black people were slaves. Some were prospering in trade and leading somewhat normal lives for the times in the free states. During the period of slavery, free blacks made up about one-tenth of the entire black population. In 1860 there were almost 500,000 free blacks, half in the South and half in the North. They originated with former indentured servants and their descendants; free black immigrants from the West Indies; and blacks freed by individual slaveowners. But they were only technically free. In the North, although the free black population had some access to education and could organize, they were discriminated against in such rights as voting, property ownership, and freedom of movement. They also faced the danger of being kidnapped and enslaved. In the South, the free blacks posed a threat to the institution of slavery, and they suffered both in law and by custom many of the restrictions imposed on slaves.

The U. S. Census of that era clearly indicates that in the white population, the differences between the "haves and have nots" were extreme. The "haves" were physicians, merchants, dentists, printers, traders, lawyers, trustees; with real estate, slaves and money. All were educated. The next "class" had some form of education. They were jewelers, music professors, shoemakers, livery stable repairmen, teachers, cabinet makers, silversmiths, draymen, carriage makers. Last came the poor farmers , with no future, whose only assets were their children. Whites who were not born into money, nor had an education, literally broke their backs making a living, and had few ways out of poverty. (The most popular avenue the "have nots" used to reverse their meager existence was to marry spouses with money.) All servant positions were taken by blacks. Factories were almost non-existent in the South, and agriculture was the main source of income. Fields were worked by blacks. "Being white was the only dignity they had — so they held on until they realized being white and scratching for food did not equate."

If the Civil War had not been fought and slavery remained intact, the possible future scenario might have been that industry would head South and . . . build factories . . . buy slaves . . . house them in shacks . . . and breed future factory workers. The abuse of humans would have escalated, until, perhaps, a slave insurrection would have occurred. The poor whites would still have no jobs and no way to escape their poverty; therefore, the issue was economics, as well as morality.

10

The tragic break was coming . . . the North and South were parting. Contributing to, and leading up to this schism, were the Missouri Compromise of 1820, the Dred Scott Decision of 1857, and Abolitionist sentiment in the North. In 1859 white abolitionist John Brown led a band of raiders in a night raid against a federal arsenal at Harpers Ferry, Virginia to instigate the uprising of Virginia slaves. The raiders executed five pro-slavery settlers at Pottawatomie Creek, but Brown was captured and later hanged. Although abolitionists denounced Brown's raid as an act of terrorism, many Northerners were angered by his hanging. And the South was shocked at the suggestion of a slave uprising. There had been previous slave revolts, but few successful, as most plots were invariably betrayed. The slave revolt that was perhaps most frightening to white slaveowners was the one led by Nat Turner in Southampton, Virginia in 1830, in which about 60 whites were killed before the conspirators were captured.

Whatever the cause . . . slavery . . . states' rights . . . tariffs. . . poverty and/or prosperity . . . politics . . . the Civil War had finally come. December 20, 1860 marked the first break that was to widen into a complete split in the nation. At a Charleston convention, South Carolina voted to secede from the Union. Six days later, Major Robert Anderson moved his Union troops from Fort Moultrie to Fort Sumter in Charleston Harbor.

On March 4, 1861, this grim eve of the Civil War, Abraham Lincoln waited to be inaugurated as sixteenth President of the United States. His new political party—the Republicans—adopted anti-slavery and Unionism as its creed. This set the stage for the final confrontation, although even before he took office, Southern states began seceding from the Union.

The closing phrases of Lincoln's "House Divided" speech at his inauguration rang with the declaration: "I do not expect the house to fall; but I do expect it will cease to be divided. It will become all one thing, or all the other." On January 1, 1863, President Lincoln issued the Emancipation Proclamation that declared forever free those slaves within the Confederacy.

The Civil War—the war that cost more American lives than all the other wars of the United States put together—began when troops loyal to the new Confederacy fired on Union Troops at Fort Sumter, South Carolina. Lincoln won re-election to the Presidency in 1864, as Union military triumphs heralded an end to the war. At war's end, on April 9, 1865, General Robert E. Lee surrendered to General Ulysses S. Grant in Virginia. On April 14 at Ford's Theater in Washington, President Lincoln was assassinated by actor John Wilkes Booth. The last Union troops would not leave the South until 1877, after a long and difficult period of Southern Reconstruction.

The Thirteenth Amendment to the Constitution abolished slavery in the United States and all its territories. The resolution for the amendment was adopted by Congress on January 31, 1865 and ratified by 27 states on December 18. The Thirteenth Amendment specified: "Neither slavery nor involuntary servitude, except as punishment for crime whereof the party shall have been duly convicted, shall exist within the United States, or any place subject to their jurisdiction."

Chapter 3

Joseph Clark
Freedom and Exodus

In giving freedom to the slave, we assure freedom to the free,—honourable alike in what we give and what we preserve.

Abraham Lincoln
Annual message to Congress
1 Dec. 1862

The Civil War ends — FREEDOM FOR THE SLAVES!! Six-year-old Joseph, our great-grandfather, now has a surname. His name becomes Joseph Clark. Upon freeing their slaves, the plantation owners give their last name to the black slaves. This helps to explain why the black community, on the whole, to this day suffers a lack of consistency and cohesiveness. Blacks consist of many divergent African tribes, with diverse gene pools. For survival they formed plantation families, and upon freedom took their slaveholder's surname, thus, once again perpetrating another tribe.

At the end of the Civil War, many plantation owners obtain legal permission to retain some of their former slaves as freed workers. Many of the former slaves are without support. These include the elderly and women with young children with no males to support them. The plantation owners' largesse assists many of their former slaves during Southern Reconstruction. But this is not for William Clark and his family.

As a trusted slave William Clark, Joseph's father, is a drayman for the Clark Plantation and has the opportunity to visit different parts of the state as he hauls goods on a dray (a low sturdy cart with detachable sides for carrying heavy loads). By not being isolated at the plantation, he has the opportunity to become aware of events that are happening throughout the country. As a visionary, William wants to leave the plantation and start a new life for his wife and young family. He realizes that education is the key to a good and secure future. (At the time, 95% of the country is illiterate.)

But where to go? Now that the Clarks are free, William wants to take them to an area that promises them a better life. He is aware that General Joe Wheeler won a battle for the Confederates outside of Covington, Georgia, but he is also aware that the Union took control of all of Tennessee. There, he hears in his travels as a drayman, are opportunities for work and promises of schooling for the recently freed blacks. *The Clark Family now begins its journey from Georgia up Route 75 to Chattanooga, Tennessee and a new life.*

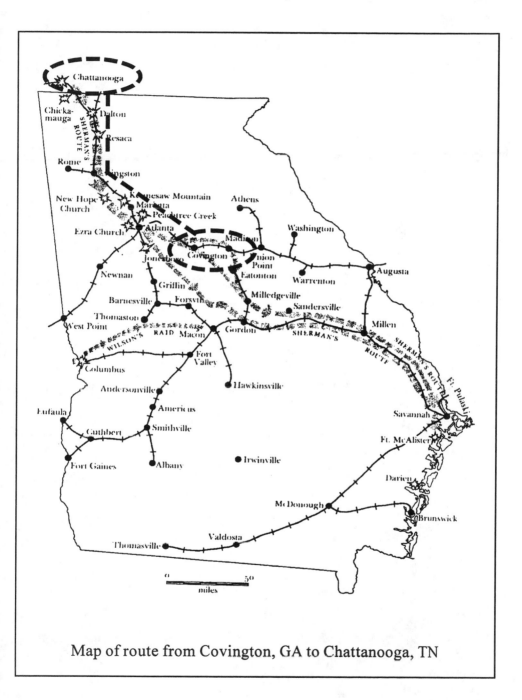

Map of route from Covington, GA to Chattanooga, TN

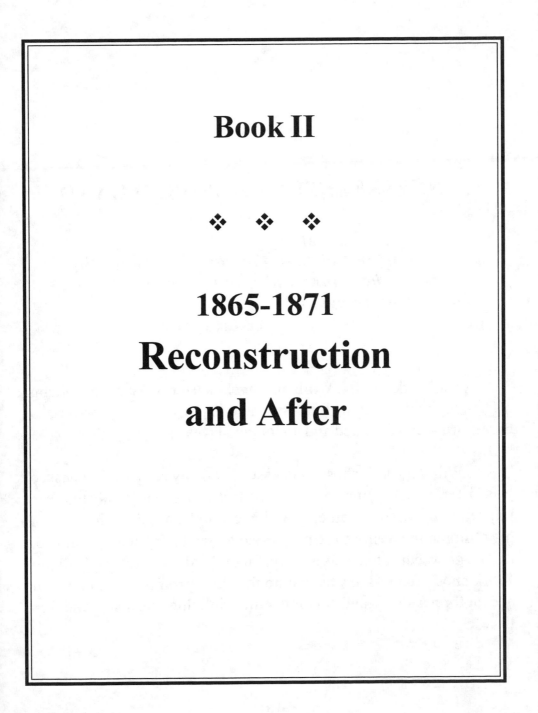

Book II

❖   ❖   ❖

1865-1871
Reconstruction
and After

Chapter 4

TENNESSEE: THE PROMISED LAND

"You can't change the past. You can only embrace the future and give it your best. It is time to begin again."

Tom Clancy "Politika"

The Clark Family: William, Angelina, Henry, Mary, and young Joseph are now living in Tennessee and happily looking forward to the future -- emancipated and no longer slaves.

William Clark chose Tennessee for many reasons. Tennessee was offering schooling to the recently freed slaves, and this was important to Joseph's father. By his example, William instilled in his children the desire to strive to rise above their "station" in life, and he knew education was a powerful tool. Another reason William Clark chose Tennessee was that he felt this "promised land" would accept former slaves and not hinder them in achieving a new and free life.

East Tennessee always sided with the Union. In 1861, they voted by an overwhelming majority against withdrawing the State from the Union. East Tennessee was a thorn in the side of the Harris administration at Nashville, and the Davis administration at Richmond. It has been estimated that thirty-five thousand East Tennesseans fought for the preservation of the Union under the flag of the United States.

East Tennessee remained a strong Union section of the South for perhaps two reasons: topography and climate. The Eastern part of Tennessee was cut off by high mountains from easy contact with the rest of the world, and became separate from the rest of the State in social structure and economic interest. This region was a land of independent landowners who tilled their small farms themselves. Few owned slaves, therefore, the plantation system of the regions where large slaveholders were the dominate element of society never flourished in East Tennessee. East Tennessee did not yield to the growing demand for Southern independence in 1861 as did most of Middle and West Tennessee.

After the conclusion of the Civil War, Republicans in Congress prepared the Fourteenth Amendment to the Constitution of the United States: The Enfranchisement of the Negro. The Amendment's first section, "gave citizenship to negroes, and denied to any State the right to abridge the privileges and immunities of citizens or to deprive any person of life, liberty, or property without due process of law, or to deny to any person the equal protection of the laws." The second section "provided for a reduction in the Congressional representation of any State that should not enfranchise the negro." The third section "denied the right to hold office to any of the leading supporters of the Confederacy." The fourth section "prohibited the payment by the United States or any State of debts incurred in support of any rebellion against the United States or of any claims for the loss or emancipation of slaves." Of the former states of the Confederacy, Tennessee was the only one in 1866 to ratify the Fourteenth Amendment, and a resolution was quickly passed by Congress that declared her restored to her normal relations to the Union, and Tennessee Senators and Representatives were permitted to take their seats in Congress. Thus, Tennessee alone, of former Confederate States, escaped a return to military rule and reconstruction according to the plan that Congressional Radicals put into operation in the following year in spite of President Andrew Johnson's opposition. *In 1868 the Fourteenth Amendment granted citizenship to blacks.*

In 1870, five years after the Civil War ended, the Fifteenth Amendment to the U.S. Constitution gave black men the right to vote. However, being able to exercise that right was a different matter for black men for a long time. In the late 1800s and through the early 20th century, blacks were often discouraged from voting. States such as Mississippi instituted a poll tax, literacy tests, and other measures to prevent blacks from voting. Blatant intimidation was used as well. In 1868, 40 black men who tried to vote in Orlando, Florida, were beaten by a white man with a bullwhip and driven out of town before the sheriff came to their rescue. Race relations and voting rights in Orange County, Florida, hit an all-time low in November, 1920 when a riot erupted in Ocoee on Election Day after a black man tried to vote. (Both black and white women were unable to vote until the Nineteenth Amendment was ratified 50 years later.) *It wasn't until October 3, 1950 that Orlando, Florida held its first primary election that was open to men (and women) of all races.*

20

Chapter 5

CITIZENSHIP AND THE RIGHT TO VOTE

One man shall have one vote.
John Cartwright

During the summer of 1866 there was a contest waged between President Andrew Johnson and the Republicans to secure victory in the Congressional elections of that year. In many parts of Middle and West Tennessee fewer whites registered to vote than did blacks. An example was Davidson County, when in early June only 612 whites registered to vote, while 1,136 blacks registered. Some of the black Republicans became unruly and were insolent to the disfranchised whites. To great numbers of whites it seemed an outrage that any former slave should vote no matter how many had registered.

Leaders of both the Conservative faction and Radical faction of the Republican parties feared rioting and bloodshed on election day. In Knoxville, the black members of the Union League were advised: "On the day of election, drink no liquor, offer no insults to any class of men, white or colored, and demean yourselves in all other respects as good citizens. . . Show to the world that you hold the public peace as paramount, human life as sacred, and the supremacy of the law as of the first importance." (As recorded in *Tennessee, A History, 1673-1932*.) Election day, August 1, passed peacefully and the Republicans were overwhelmingly successful at the polls.

But, however the election turned out, and despite claims of foul by the opposing parties, the black was proud of his vote. One countryman brought his wife with him when he voted and said, "'She can't vote, but bress God, I fotch her long to see dot I kin, I golly." (*Tennessee, A History, 1673-1932.*)

Jim Crow Laws (Jim Crow is thought to be an old nickname for Black Americans, popularized in a song), or segregation laws, first developed in a few Northern states in the early 1800s, were adopted by many Southern states in the late 1800s. These segregation laws required that whites and blacks use separate public facilities. No detail was too small. At one time, for example, Oklahoma required that whites and blacks use separate telephone booths. Arkansas specified separate gambling tables, and many courts provided separate Bibles for swearing in witnesses. Several Southern states adopted grandfather clauses and other Jim Crow laws that deprived blacks of their voting rights.

Chapter 6
A NEW LIFE

The difference between the impossible and
the possible lies in man's determination.

Anonymous

Tennessee gave William Clark the right to vote for the first time in his life. How proud he was!! The Clark family celebrated true emancipation and was thriving. William, now 38, was working as a drayman. Angelina, 41, was "keeping house." Mary, 13, and William, Jr. (known as Isaac), 4, were "at home." Joseph, 10, was working as a dray driver with his father, and attending school. Proudly, Isaac was the first member of William Clark's family to be born (1867) in freedom. The Clark's oldest son, 26-year-old Henry, was now married, had a family, and was also living in Tennessee working as a farm laborer. (According to the 1870 Census of Chattanooga, Tennessee.)

William Clark was not only a visionary, but very frugal, as well. His net worth, listed in the U.S. Census of 1870, was listed at $400. This was truly amazing for a former slave. He and his family had only been free for five years. Subsequent chapters will show that son Joseph Clark was also very frugal, and this stood him in good stead in future years as he pursued his quest for prosperity and a successful future. Great-granddaughter, Gloria Fenton Magbie, was delighted to discover that she is following in her ancestors' footsteps, and her frugality is a result of her genes.

23

Chapter 7

THE PURSUIT OF EXCELLENCE
Education For All

Education has for its object the formation of character.

Herbert Spencer

Ever since their arrival in Tennessee in 1865, William Clark's children, Joseph and Mary, attended school. Not only was it unusual for blacks to have an education, but it was extremely unusual for a girl child to attend school. William Clark wanted all his children to have an education and believed that "Education was your key to respectability and a chance to better your life." Son, Joseph, now 11 years old, and attending school, supplemented the family income by working as a drayman. Unfortunately the educational opportunity came too late to be of use to older brother, Henry, who was now married and supporting a family.

Schools were conducted in headmasters' homes, log buildings (one room), sod huts with wildflowers blooming out of the sod bricks, or whatever space could be acquired. Parents paid from a few pennies a day, up to a couple of hundred dollars a year, to educate their children. Students were taught reading, writing, and ciphering (arithmetic). For some students, schooling consisted of a few days a year; others perhaps 12 weeks a year. Books were highly prized, cherished, and re-read many times. These "treasures" were committed to memory and quoted many times over to those who could not read and were illiterate. Imagine how impressed these former slaves would be! Imagine how the literate former slave would feel to be able to read! To be able "to feel a little taller!"

In an interview given to the Associated Press and published in *USA Today*: "Mary Rose Adair glances out her living-room window, past the grassy plateau and dozens of oak trees and sees a place where she embraced the value of education. 'I consider the ground over there sacred ground,' she said, looking at the last red-brick building left from Brainerd Institute, Chester, South Carolina." Presbyterians founded Brainerd Institute in a log cabin in 1866 to educate freed slaves. It later became South Carolina's largest and oldest school for blacks and a feeder school for predominantly black Benedict College, Johnson C. Smith University, and Howard University. Brainerd became a junior college in 1934 and continued to take elementary and high-school students. It finally closed its doors in 1939 as more public schools became available for blacks. "This is my heart. This is my life. This is my heritage," said Adair. She was one of Brainerd's last graduates before it closed in 1939.

It was not until 1954, however, in *Brown v. Board of Education, Topeka, Kansas*, that the United States Supreme Court declared the segregation of races in the public schools to be unconstitutional, and in succeeding years struck at other aspects of segregation in the South.

Chapter 8

TROUBLE IN PARADISE
The Rise of the Ku Klux Klan

The better day, the worse deed.
Matthew Henry

The Republicans were greatly strengthened in their control of Tennessee as a result of the election of 1867. The Republican victory had been as impressive as it was because of the almost unanimous support of the newly enfranchised blacks, even though the Conservatives, deliberately but unsuccessfully, sought to win the votes of the blacks during this election. There was a definite division among the opponents of the Republicans on the question of black suffrage. And the *Chattanooga Union* voiced the demands of many Conservatives: "We shall lose nothing by a bold avowal of our unqualified opposition to negro suffrage, and of our intention when we come into power, as we shall surely do, of taking away from the negroes the power of ruling white men, which has been given them by demagogues for selfish purposes . . . ."

In bitter disappointment at the way black voters had cast their ballots almost as a unit for Republican candidates, many from the white majority were becoming desperate and increasingly hostile to the black race. In retaliation, many black workmen were discharged by white employers. The feeling against the white Republican leaders and the blacks was so intense in some sections of the State of Tennessee following the election that State troops, due to be disbanded, remained in Jackson, Trenton, Nashville, McMinnville, Pulaski, and Lewisburg. However, after the troops were disbanded, disorder in Middle and West Tennessee increased, and a race riot occurred in Pulaski in January, 1868. Two blacks were killed, five wounded; and one white man was seriously injured.

In Pulaski in May/ June of 1866, a small group of young men, former members of the Confederate Army, organized a social club solely to "provide entertainment for themselves." This was to be a secret society, and they choose the Greek word *Kuklos,* meaning a circle, as the name of their club. This was readily transformed into Ku Klux Klan. Although the Pulaski Klan was originally organized solely for the amusement of its members, they found that the "superstitious and ignorant negroes" could be profoundly influenced by the Klan's mysterious ceremonies and the regalia of its members. Local "dens" of the Klan were formed in towns and country districts near Pulaski, and eventually spread into other states. Thus, the Ku Klux Klan became a body of regulators and the most important manifestation of the bitter opposition of the disfranchised whites to the policy of the Republicans, that sought to place the blacks in a position of superiority to the ex-Confederate majority. Agitation and conflict started appearing with the intimidation of the black voters and the burning of schools that taught blacks. The Freedman Bureau, which was supposed to help this transition, was in itself ill-managed and corrupt.

The Clark family lived in Chattanooga (Middle Tennessee), approximately 150 miles from Pulaski, where the Klan originated and spread it tentacles of hate toward blacks. The patriarch, William Clark, weighed his options, and decided to move the family back to Georgia for their safety and progression to a better life for his loved ones.

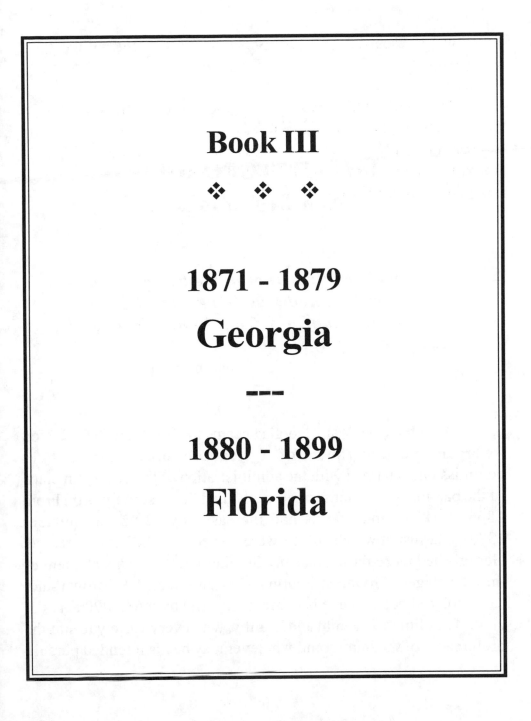

Book III

❖ ❖ ❖

1871 - 1879

Georgia

1880 - 1899

Florida

Chapter 9

1871 - 1879 GEORGIA
New Beginnings

Hope springs eternal in the human breast;
Man never Is, but always To be blest. The soul,
uneasy, and confin'd from home, rests and
expatiates in a life to come . . .

Alexander Pope

After the Civil War, Georgia became the first State in the Union to organize a Department of Agriculture, presided over by a commissioner charged with the administration of the office. In place of the baronial plantations, small well-tilled farms sprung forth. From 1868 to 1873, small farms had increased by 32,824, to number 138,626 farms, of which 76,451 were owned, and the balance rented. Georgia had more farms than any Southern State. In a statement of the advantages of living in Georgia, Governor Joseph E. Brown said: "The colored people have become thrifty and own 680,000 acres of land. The climate is genial and healthy, with every variety to suit the preferences of the immigrant, whatever may be his intended pursuit.

In free education, the State is marching apace with the age." In 1871, white pupils numbered 42,914 and black pupils numbered 6,664. By 1878, whites numbered 137,217; and blacks 72,655.

Thus . . . Georgia offered new hope for the Clark family. Patriarch William, always striving to improve his family's existence, moved them to Atlanta where they prospered and were reared. Although they experienced joy in their new life, it was mingled with great sorrow. Their beloved daughter and sister, Mary, died in Georgia in 1870 at the young age of 13. (As listed in the Georgia 1870 Mortality Census.)

Joseph was particularly devastated. There was only a two-year difference between them, and Mary had essentially raised him. They had both been born in slavery. They had both moved with their family to freedom in Tennessee. They had gone to school for the first time together in Tennessee. They had both headed to Georgia with dreams and hope for the future. Matriarch Angelina Clark also died in Georgia in the 1870s. (As listed in the Georgia Census.) However, both Mary and Angelina died as freewomen, and not slaves.

The Clark family now consisted of widower William, and his three sons: Henry, the eldest; Joe; and Isaac, the youngest. They all worked diligently and were very enterprising. Recognizing the importance of education for their people, these young men assisted in building the Morris-Brown College (A.M.E.) in Atlanta in 1879.

Chapter 10

JOSEPH CLARK STARTS A FAMILY

*No one goes his way alone; All that we send
into the lives of others, comes back into our own.*
Edwin Markholm

In the early 1870s in Georgia, Joseph married Julia Hightower, a Blackfoot Indian. They had three daughters. In memory of Mary, his beloved sister, Joseph and Julia gave each child a name beginning with the letter "M." Their daughter, Mattie, was born in 1872; Mande in 1876; and Mamie in 1879. Joseph Clark, Julia and the children moved from Atlanta to Thomas City, Georgia, on Florida's border, in the early 1880s. (As indicated in the Thomas, Georgia, Census of 1880.) There are many Clarks and Hightowers still living in the area.

Mattie, the oldest child of Julia and Joe Clark, would regale her children and grandchildren with stories of her Blackfoot Indian mother. "My mother had the most beautiful hair you have ever seen. It was so long, that she could sit on it!"

Their tranquil life was shattered, however, when Julia Hightower Clark became ill. Mattie, Mande and Mamie were separated and sent to live among the Clark family members. On the 1880 Maitland, Florida Census, Joseph indicates that he is married, not widowed; confirming that Julia died the latter part of 1880 or 1881, after a long illness.

The Blackfoot Indians - Our Ancestors

There were many Indians (listed as M - Mulattos) on the Census Sheets in Georgia. Their origin dates back to intermarriages with blacks. Joseph Clark's wife, Julia Hightower was a Blackfoot Indian living in Georgia. The original Blackfoot Tribe was based in Canada and used the Old North Trail from Canada as an Interstate into the United States. In an article by Peter Stark, "The Old North Trail," published in the *Smithsonian Magazine*, the author writes: "Imagine a mountain ridge that snakes like a knobbly spine all the way from the frozen Canadian Arctic down to the deserts of Mexico. 'The Backbone of the World,' the Blackfoot Indians called what we know as the Rocky Mountains and the Continental Divide." On one side of the spine lies the Pacific Ocean, and on the other the Great Plains. The Blackfoot Indians followed a footpath that ran along the base of the mountains, a "shoreline" between the mountains and plains. They "ran" on it for 2,000 or 3,000 miles.

Peter Stark continues, "The earliest humans who crossed from Asia may have walked this route when they migrated south to populate the Americas at least 15,000 years ago. This would make it the oldest and longest trail on the continent." Early explorers' accounts actually mention Indian journeys of thousands of miles along the Old North Trail.

33

Although the Blackfoot, renowned as fierce warriors and expert buffalo hunters, had once controlled an enormous sweep of the Great Plains along the eastern front of the Rocky Mountains in today's Alberta and Montana, they had been decimated by disease, encroaching settlers, and the wholesale slaughter of their herds by white hunters by the late 19th century. However, Keith Thurlkill, Historic Trail Coordinator for the U.S. Forest Service, says, "Truth is, people have walked everywhere," and many of their progeny settled south of Canada. Dennis Stanford of the Smithsonian's National Museum of Natural History believes the migrations occurred gradually via both the Pacific Coast and various interior routes. Thus, Julia Hightower's ancestors could have walked the Old North Trail and veered left toward Georgia.

1880 - 1899 - Florida

Chapter 11

JOSEPH CLARK BECOMES A "BIG MAN"
Maitland

*It's not the way the wind blows in life that
makes the difference; it's the way we set our sails
in the wind and thus allow the wind to guide
and direct us.* Fr. Paul Keenan

Joseph E. Clark was always looking for ways to "move on" and provide a better life for his family. He was 21 years old and an educated black man—very unique for his time: a hard worker and very gentlemanly. Although his family was still living in Georgia, Joseph went South into Florida to explore new job opportunities. Impressed with Joseph's industriousness and drive were Captain Josiah C. Eaton, a retired United States Navy Paymaster originally from Maine who hired Joseph to work in his groves; Lewis Lawrence, wealthy industrialist of Utica N.Y., and Winter resident of Maitland; and Isaac Vanderpool, businessman and owner of a citrus packing company and orange groves in Maitland. These three influential men became Clark's mentors. The U.S. Census of 1880 lists Joseph E. Clark as living in Josiah C. Eaton's house and working in Eaton's Orange Groves. He is also listed as a married man (not widowed). Joseph, after the death of his first wife, Julia Hightower, was married for a second time in 1882 to a woman named Martha, six years his senior. They did not have any children. Joseph's three children joined him in Florida after his marriage to Martha.

Maitland, Florida

Lake Maitland was named after Captain William Seton Maitland, a career Army officer descended from Scottish noblemen, who served in the area in 1838 during the Second Seminole War. At one time it was a shopping center for the infant villages of Orlando and Winter Park, but was soon outstripped in population by its younger neighbors. In 1876 Lake Maitland was laid out as a town by Isaac Vanderpool, Henry S. Kedney and brothers George and Richard Packwood.

In 1884, a group of Union veterans decided to incorporate the settlement, but discovered they did not have the required 30 registered voters. They, thus, induced blacks employed in the groves to become residents. Blacks soon outnumbered the whites and were elected to office. Clark thrived and became so involved in the politics of Maitland that he served for one year as a Town Marshall. When Maitland was incorporated on July 17, 1885, he was one of the signers—a great honor for the young black man. At that time, the

36

Florida Census of 1885 shows J. E. Clark's holdings at $1500.00—3 acres planted and 8 acres woodlands.

Josiah C. Eaton was Incorporated Maitland's first mayor, but it soon became apparent that the voting power of the whites was being diluted with too many black voters. Shortly after the Civil War, recently freed slaves moved to Central Florida in search of work. They cleared land and planted vegetables and citrus groves, built houses, worked on Central Florida's first railroad, and were domestic servants in wealthy families' households. Added to this problem, blacks were building shanties and doing their wash in Lake Lily (St. John's Hole) which was not conducive to the establishment of an upscale town. An unique solution was proposed—let blacks buy land a couple of miles from Maitland and establish their own town.

(No. 1011—NEW SERIES—JANUARY 1, 1884.)

(LOCATION PAPER)

MAY 16 1889

Post Office Department,

OFFICE OF THE FIRST ASSISTANT P. M. GENERAL,

WASHINGTON, D. C., _May 7_, 188 9

SIR: Before the Postmaster General decides upon the application for the establishment of a post office at _Eatonville_, County of _Orange_, State of _Fla._, it will be necessary for you to carefully answer the subjoined questions, get a neighboring postmaster to certify to the correctness of the answers, and return the location paper to the Department, addressed to me. If the site selected for the proposed office should not be on any mail route now under contract, only a "Special Office" can be established there, to be supplied with mail from some convenient point on the nearest mail route by a special carrier, for which service a sum equal to two-thirds of the amount of the salary of the postmaster at such office will be paid.

You should inform the contractor, or person performing service for him, of this application, and require him to execute the inclosed certificate as to the practicability of supplying the proposed office with mail, and return the same to the Department.

Very respectfully,

A. E. Stinson

First Assistant Postmaster General.

To Mr. _J. E. Clark_

care of the Postmaster of _Lake Maitland_, who will please forward to him.

STATEMENT.

The proposed office to be called _Eatonville_

Select a short name for the proposed office, which, when written, will not resemble the name of any other post office in the State.

It will be situated in the _S 1/2_ of Section _36_, Township _21_ (North or South)

Range _29_ (East or West), _East_, in the County of _Orange_, State of _Florida_

It will be on or near route No. _____, being the route from _Sanford to Orlando_ to _Tampa_, on which the mail is now carried _6 Seven_ times per week.

The contractor's name is _South Florida Rail Road_

Will it be directly on this route?—Ans. _No_

If not, how far from, and on which side of it?—Ans. _About One and a Quarter Mile S_

How much will it INCREASE the travel of the mail one way each trip?—Ans. _none_

Where will the mail leave the present route to supply the proposed office?—Ans. _At Lake Maitland_

Where intersect the route again?—Ans. _T Lum to L Maitland_

What post office will be left out by this change?—Ans. _none_

If not on any route, is a "Special Office" wanted?—Ans. _Yes_ To be supplied from _Lake Maitland_

The name of the nearest office to the proposed one, on the same route, is _Lake Maitland_

its distance is _One & One qr miles_ miles in a _North Easterly_ direction from the proposed office.

The name of the nearest office on the same route, on the other side, is _Winter Park_

its distance _Two_ miles in a _South East_ direction from the proposed office.

The name of the nearest office to the proposed one, not on this route, is _Maitland Green_

distance by the most direct road _five_ miles in a _South West_ direction from the proposed office.

The name of the most prominent river near it is _St. Johns_

The name of the nearest creek is _Wekiwa_

The proposed office will be _16 or 17_ miles from said river, on the _East_ side of it, and will be _three_ miles from said nearest creek, on the _East_ side of it

The name of the nearest railroad is _1/2 mile from track_

Title excerpt from the application of Joseph E. Clark
for Postmaster of Eatonville (circa 1889)

Chapter 12

A DREAM COMES TRUE
Eatonville

I dream'd in a dream I saw a city invincible
to the attacks of the whole of the rest of the earth,
I dream'd that was the new city of Friends.
Walt Whitman

Joseph Clark had always dreamed of a town established for blacks and by blacks; and there was no holding him back now.

Initially, establishing this township did not at first appear promising. "The white land owners were unable or unwilling to sell them any tract large enough for that purpose." (Eatonville Historic District.) In 1883, support and guidance for the new town came from Isaac Vanderpool; Josiah C. Eaton, who sold land to Clark; and Lewis Lawrence who bought an extra 22 acres from Josiah C. Eaton and gave 12 acres to Clark and 10 acres to the Trustees of the African Methodist Episcopal Church.

On August 15, 1887, 22 years out of slavery, a group of 27 black men, including Joseph E. Clark, met in the Oddfellows Hall, a building donated to the new community by Lewis Lawrence, and voted on the question of incorporating the Town of Eatonville in Orange County, Florida. This was in response to a legal notice advertised in the *Maitland Courier*. These men, all residing within the boundaries of the proposed town, voted unanimously to incorporate the municipality. Eatonville, named for Captain Josiah Eaton of Maitland, is recognized today as the oldest incorporated all-black town in the United States.

In the 1887 incorporation document of the Town of Eatonville, Orange County, Florida, as catalogued in the Orange County Regional History Center of Central Florida: "The original city limits include the SE 1/4 of the NE 1/4 and the NE 1/4 of the SE 1/4 of Section 35, and the 'SW of the SW' of the NW1/4, the NW 1/4 of the NW 1/4 of the SW 1/4, and the North 149 feet of the SW 1/4 of the NW 1/4 of Section 26, Township 21 South, Range 29 East, all lying in Orange County, Florida, and consisting of approximately 112 acres."

The signers of the "Incorporation Papers of the Town of Eatonville in Orange County, Florida, August 15, 1887" were: Simon Bevin, A. J. Bird, C. H. Boger, Louis Brazell, J. B. Brazell, Matthew B. Brazell, Richard Butler, Smart Bynum, F. Caraway, J. E. Clark, Thomas Clemmon, David Gelder, E. L. Horn, J. R. Johnson, Anderson Lawson, Joseph Lindsay, T. J. Pender, George Oats, L. Sewall, E. J. Shines, C. S. Sizemore, Elloy Smith, John Suman, J. T. Taylor, W. T. Thomas, Joseph Walker, J. N. Watson, Richard Weston, and Ishmael Williams. (Note: Of the 29 men listed, only 27 actually signed the incorporation papers.)

40

J. E. Clark, M. B. Brazell, David Gelder, E. J. Shine and E. L. Horn were elected Aldermen. The first Mayor was Columbus H. Boger. Other elected officials were: J. R. Johnson, Clerk; W. T. Thomas, Marshall; J. B. Brazell, Tax Assessor; J. N. Watson, Collector; L. Brazell, Treasurer. Town Council members were J. B. Brazell, M. Brazell, David Gelder, Lewis Sewell, Frank Caraway, Smart Bynum, Ishmael Williams, C. H. Boger, and J. E. Clark.

Establishing the township took enormous courage for these black men. When blacks declared themselves as voters, they became targets of the violence that was prevalent at the time to stop them from voting. It took 80 years for the blacks to get voting rights in Orlando, Florida. Although women of all races were unable to vote in the United States at this time, they still had a voice through their husbands, and many women claimed their husband's vote as their own. The women were not powerless, and voiced their opinions vehemently; often withholding food and favors unless their husbands voted their way.

In an article from *Documents from Orange County Regional History Center of Central Florida*, Joseph E. Clark is mentioned very prominently: "The property held by Clark and the St. Lawrence Church of Maitland is thought to be the first property procured for the purpose of establishing a new black township in Florida. The additional land was bought by Joseph Clark, who would be one of the first mayors of Eatonville. As Frank M. Otey said in his book, *Eatonville, Florida, A Brief History*, "If it is true that every town should have a founding father, then Eatonville's should certainly be Joseph E. Clark." According to the *Orlando Sentinel*, Sunday, October 20, 1991, "Joseph subdivided the land and sold off lots to

41

black families, many of whom worked as farmhands, grove workers or housekeepers in nearby Maitland, Winter Park or Orlando." They also published a picture of Clark in front of his general store, with the caption: "After buying land, Clark built a general store that became a social center in Eatonville . . .."

In an appeal to new residents, J. E. Clark advertised in the *Maitland Courier* that there were "Building Lots for Sale in Eatonville, Florida."

Appearing in a notice on the front page of the January 22, 1889 edition of the city's weekly newspaper the *Eatonville Speaker* was the following:

"Colored people of the United States: Solve the great race problem by securing a home in Eatonville, Florida, a Negro City governed by Negroes"

Following was detailed information on the location, describing the area surrounding Eatonville, and history of the town. The article also stated "Six years have passed and to-day Eatonville is an incorporated city of between two and three hundred population with a Mayor, Board of Aldermen and all the necessary adjuncts of a full-fledged city, all colored, and Not A White Family in the whole city. Five and ten tracts can be bought for five and ten dollars an acre, according to location and improvements. In Eatonville, lots to actual settlers (colored): 44 x 100, can be bought for thirty-five dollars cash; and fifty on time. For further particulars address: J. E. Clark, Eatonville, Orange Co., FLA."

Joseph Clark and his family prospered in Eatonville. Not only was Joseph one of the founding fathers, but by 1889, he was Mayor of Eatonville; Business Manager of the *Eatonville Speaker* from 1888 to November 8, 1890; Postmaster; and owner of a general store. His listing on the front page of the *Eatonville Speaker* advertised:

CLARK & CO.,
DEALERS IN
STAPLE — AND — FANCY

Prior to the establishment of a Post Office in Eatonville in 1889, mail for the area was delivered to the Lake Maitland Post Office. Joseph E. Clark applied for and became the first Postmaster of Eatonville on May 25, 1889. Matthew B. Brazell became Postmaster on September 7, 1907, followed by Sylvia V. Pindar on September 18, 1908. The last Postmaster of Eatonville was Hiram B. Lester, who became Postmaster on May 31, 1916. Service to Eatonville was discontinued on May 5, 1918, and as per U. S. Postmaster, Washington, D.C., all of Eatonville's mail was forwarded to Maitland. Postal services were re-established in later years and continue to the present.

In 1891, newspaper articles started appearing regarding the town. The *New York Sun* carried a lengthy article praising the whole concept of Eatonville.

"Eatonville, situated just two miles and a half north of Winter Park is a town, incorporated by colored people, inhabited by colored people and the officers from the Mayor down are colored men. It

is a strange thing in the history of our country, yet such does exist.There, exist a government by men only partially educated, who are carrying out their laws with as much strictness as anywhere in the Country. Leaving the government and taking the business - we find Eatonville has these stores, which proprietors carry groceries, dry goods, crockery and almost every other line of goods carried in any first class store in much larger towns."

Five years after Eatonville was incorporated, Captain Josiah Eaton, mentor and benefactor of J. E. Clark died in Altamonte, Florida in 1892. Captain Eaton's tomb, with an anchor and rope (signifying his Naval background) carved on it, is in the Maitland Cemetery and reads:

**JOSIAH EATON
BORN GALIAS, MAINE, 1827
DIED ALTAMONTE, FLORIDA, 1892**

HE LOVED HIS FELLOWMEN

Joseph Clark was prosperous and flourishing in Eatonville; however, he suffered some personal misfortunes. Clark lost two close relatives within three years. In 1896 his eldest brother, Henry Clark died. Henry had joined Joseph in Florida and worked side by side with him in Eatonville. In 1899, our Grandmother, Mattie Clark, the eldest of Joseph Clark's three daughters left Eatonville for Georgia. She often mentioned to her children and grandchildren that she could not stand the "meanness" of her stepmother, Martha Clark. Sadly, Joseph Clark never saw Mattie again.

Evidently, Clark's two remaining daughters, Mamie and Mande moved to Atlanta, Georgia, as well. Over the years, even after Grandmother moved to New York, she would often go back to Georgia to visit her sisters. Mamie remained in Georgia; Mande moved and lost contact with her family.

Calhoun Dining Hall at the Robert Hungerford Normal and Industrial School (circa 1940) Photo courtesy of Louise Franklin.

Building A Community

Our todays and yesterdays are the blocks with which we build.

Longfellow

Chapter 13

Education in Eatonville
The Robert Hungerford School

Education makes us what we are.
C. A. Helvetius
**"One institution that helped insure the success of Eatonville
was the Robert Hungerford Industrial School."**
Eatonville Historic District
Orange County, Florida.

In 1887, Dr. Robert Hungerford, a young white physician from Seymour, Connnecticut spent a winter with his parents, Edward and Anna Hungerford in Maitland, Florida, to improve his health. While there he became interested in a group of serious-minded black youths and urged them to get all the education they could. Dr. Hungerford also gave free professional services to a black youth who was ill with typhoid fever. The Doctor contracted the fever and died on September 22, 1888 at the young age of twenty-six. Dr. Hungerford was a graduate of the famous College of Physicians and Surgeons of New York City.

Joseph Clark and other community leaders appealed to Booker T. Washington, founder of the Tuskegee Institute in Alabama, to assist the new town of Eatonville in the establishment of a school or academy for the education of black children in the community and elsewhere in Florida. Russell C. Calhoun and his wife, Mary, both graduates of Tuskegee Institute, were sent by Washington in 1889 to set up the new school—two years after the incorporation of the town.

The group of young blacks befriended by Dr. Hungerford requested the new school be named the Robert Hungerford School in grateful memory of the young physician whose sincere, magnetic friendship that winter in Maitland became a permanent inspiration in their lives.

An excerpt from the *Eatonville Speaker* -- June 22, 1889, states: "At a patron meeting on the 18th inst., trustees were elected for school No. 70, viz: — J. E. Clark, S. M. Mosley, M. S. Green, C. H. Boger and T. W. Taylor. Without hesitancy a choice selection to provide for the educational destiny of our town."

Using Tuskegee as their model, the Calhouns started a school that would eventually provide vocational and academic training for black students in Central Florida. According to the *Eatonville Speaker* their goal was to "teach a vocational trade or skill to black boys and girls. In addition, a good work ethic, sound morals and human values and proper social graces were

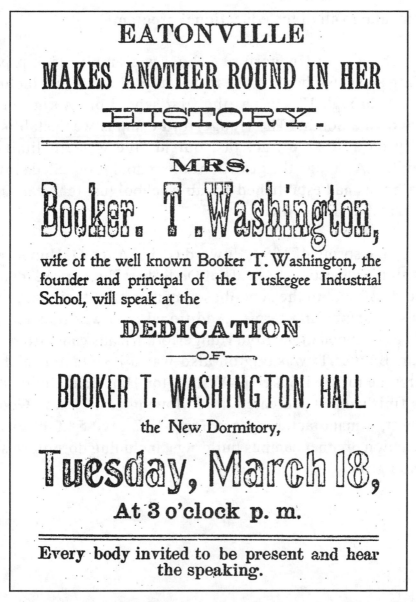

EATONVILLE
MAKES ANOTHER ROUND IN HER
HISTORY.

MRS.
Booker. T. Washington,

wife of the well known Booker T. Washington, the founder and principal of the Tuskegee Industrial School, will speak at the

DEDICATION
—OF—
BOOKER T. WASHINGTON, HALL
the New Dormitory,
Tuesday, March 18,
At 3 o'clock p. m.

Every body invited to be present and hear the speaking.

Announcement of the dedication of the Booker T. Washington Hall
at the Robert Hungerford Normal and Industrial School
(circa 1902)

fundamental to all of the educational program."

The Robert Hungerford School was an all-black private boarding and day school for the residents of the area and included Grades 4 through 12. It was the first school of its kind in the history of the South. The Hungerford campus was established initially on a 36-acre tract just outside the western limits of Eatonville. Although the growth of the school proceeded slowly, the Calhouns had established a viable school just ten years after their arrival in Eatonville.

In the spring of 1898, Edward C. and Anna D. Hungerford of Chester, Connecticut, parents of Dr. Robert Hungerford, deeded 160 acres of land to the school as a memorial to their son, to be used as a campus and farm. Additional land was donated and bought as cash donations from Hungerford friends came from near and far. Booker T. Washington also was a benefactor, and the cornerstone for the Booker T. Washington Hall was laid in 1899. It was finished and dedicated the following year. Later, George B. Cleutt, a manufacturer from Troy, NY, gave $8,000 toward construction of other campus buildings, including dormitories for boys and girls

The Girls' Basketball team at Robert Hungerford Normal
and Industrial School (circa 1940). Photo courtesy of Louise Franklin

The Boys' Basketball team at Robert Hungerford Normal
and Industrial School (circa 1940). Photo courtesy of Louise Franklin

Chapter 14

St. Lawrence A.M.E. Church

Churches have always been the mainstay and backbone of the black community and remain so to this day.

Olga Mitchell

In 1881, a small group of citizens sought a place to worship in Eatonville; however, this was at a time when blacks could not buy land since no whites would sell it to them. Lewis Lawrence, wealthy white industrialist from Utica, NY, winter resident of Maitland, and benefactor of Eatonville, came to their aid. Lawrence built an Odd Fellows Hall and the church edifice and conferred the properties to the Eatonville community. He donated 10 acres of land. The "Orange County Deed Book W-P-772, dated April 7, 1882, listed two (2) lots 50 x 100 feet, by Lewis Lawrence to: Trustees of the African Methodist Episcopal Church known as the St. Lawrence Church of Maitland, Orange County, Florida." Thus, the first Black Church of the area was born. To honor Lewis Lawrence for his generosity, the Church was renamed the Saint Lawrence A.M.E. Church. For many

The First St. Lawrence AME Church sanctuary, Eatonville, FL
(circa 1910)

years a photograph of Lawrence occupied a conspicuous position in the center of the chancel. Lawrence Avenue, now known as Kennedy Boulevard, was so named in Lewis Lawrence's honor.

In the 1900s the membership had outgrown the old church, and a larger building was considered. The old building was "rolled" across the street with the help of another interested white friend, Mrs. Whipple — the wife of Bishop Whipple of Winter Park. The old church building was converted into a library, and Mrs. Whipple kindly donated the first 150 books. The historical edifice is now a residential home.

A second church and parsonage were built in 1908 on the site of the original church. This wooden church structure deteriorated

53

The first choir at the St. Lawrence AME Church, Eatonville, FL
(circa 1940)

over the years and was replaced by the present church building which
was completed in 1974. A treasure trove of art, which was originally
housed in the second church, is mounted on the sanctuary walls. They
are eight one-of-a-kind life-size murals painted in oil on wood panel
with scenes portraying Eatonville residents in everyday settings. They
are shown reciting the 23rd Psalm in dialect typical of rural, southern
African-Americans in the early 1900s. The murals were painted by
J. Andre' Smith of Maitland (an acquaintance of Zora Neale Hurston)
and donated to the congregation around 1936.

St. Lawrence A.M.E. Church was, and has remained, a steadfast
influence in the community. Its many distinctions include being the
oldest church in the historically recognized oldest incorporated Black
municipality in the United States of America, and the church home of
more mayors than any other church in America.

Still a very active and involved member of St. Lawrence A.M.E. Church is Louise Franklin. Although the Franklin family have acreage on Lake Sybelia and live in Maitland, they have always supported and attended St. Lawrence Church. Ms. Franklin attended the church since childhood, and in 2003 published a book on the history of St. Lawrence A.M.E. Church titled *A Call to Worship*.

Chapter 15

Grand United Order of Odd Fellows Household of Ruth

We are many parts. We are all one body, and the gifts we have we are given to share. May the spirit of love make us one indeed.

Unknown

Utilizing its scenic locale, social gatherings were held at the building on the Franklin property on Lake Sybelia in Maitland. Also held at the building were meetings of the men's lodge, the Grand United Order of Odd Fellows, and the women's lodge, the Household of Ruth. These lodges were formed in the 1870s indicating that the town of Eatonville was coming together socially before its incorporation in 1887.

Joseph E. Clark was a member of the Grand United Order of Odd Fellows. He eventually became the treasurer of the Grand United Order of Odd Fellows for the State of Florida. Clark originally belonged to the Lodge in Georgia, and was a Past Most Noble Governor.

Odd Fellow members Joseph E. Clark, J. T. Taylor and J. P. Parson, were years ahead of their time when they established the women's lodge entitled Household of Ruth, on March 30, 1877. Candidate Statements were prepared by the Past Most Noble Governors on this day, asking such questions as: "What was your name before marriage? Are you married to more than one man?"

The Past Most Noble Governor was entrusted with the well-being and moral reputation of the lodge, having had thorough knowledge of laws and usages. He was the only one that could confer degrees; therefore, the men had to stay involved until one of the women worked her way up to that degree level. After having obtained their necessary degree level, the women, from March 30, 1877 on, were qualified to confer degrees without the men's involvement.

The history of the union and covenant of the Household of Ruth was founded on the friendship that existed between Ruth and her mother-in-law Naomi. Although finding themselves in a strange land and in a dangerous situation, Ruth refused to abandon Naomi: "And Ruth said, Intreat me not to leave thee, or to return from following after thee: for whither thou goest, I will go; and where thou lodgest, I will lodge: thy people *shall be* my people, and thy God my God: Where thou diest, will I die, and there will I be buried: the LORD do so to me, and more also, *if ought* but death part thee and me." (The Holy Bible, King James Version, Ruth 1:16, 17.) The foundation of the women's lodge was this type of friendship "that every true kinsman should feel for each other." The Household of Ruth continued as a lodge until the 1960s.

William C. Curtis, Worthy Grand Scribe, also wrote the *RITUAL* of the Household of Ruth, Grand United Order of Odd Fellows. In the Initial Ceremony the candidates state: "furthermore, I will by every means, in my power, patronize, encourage, support, protect, and defend in all the relations of life, by day and by night, whatever relates to the peace, happiness and prosperity of my Brothers and Sisters of the Household of Ruth, and may God help me to keep inviolate this vow and obligation."

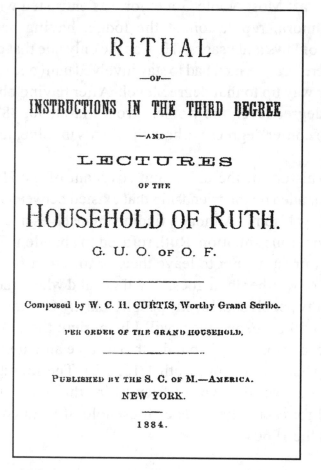

Cover page of Ritual Book Used by Household of Ruth (circa 1884)

Book IV

❖ ❖ ❖

1900-1911
Success

Life shrinks or expands in proportion to one's courage.
Anais Nin

Chapter 16

1900
EATONVILLE
The Town that Freedom Built

"The Oldest Black Incorporated Municipality in America.
It has its roots firmly planted in that blood-soaked Reconstruction soil." Anthony B. Knight, Jr.

In a Prospectus of the "Town of Eatonville," Museum Curator Anthony B. Knight, Jr., captures the essence of the times:

"On August 15, 1887, only ten years removed from Reconstruction (1863-1877), a group of twenty-seven Negro men (led by Joe Clark) convened with the purpose of founding, what would turn out to be, the first incorporated African American settlement community in the United States. Eatonville, the town born on that day, was named for a White man, Josiah Eaton, who served as mayor of the neighboring town of Maitland from which most of the future Eatonville residents originated."

Many of the residents came from as far away as South Carolina, Georgia, and Alabama. The three pillars upon which the town was founded were: family, religion and education. All-Negro towns (and more specifically, land ownership) were seen as environments in which African-Americans could thrive and flourish. It was believed that violence and harassment against the Negroes would be eliminated in an all-black town, and opportunities for self-development and community development would increase. "Determining one's political fate was not an aspect of 'town ownership' that went unnoticed by these early African-American settlers. They understood well the importance of political clout and power and worked hard to achieve them."

A case in point -- after the Civil War, the freed blacks suffered widespread discrimination, especially in the South. Jim Crow or segregation laws, first developed in a few Northern states in the early 1800s were adopted by many Southern states in the late 1800s (see Book II, Chapter 5). These segregation laws required whites and blacks to use separate public facilities; and several Southern states adopted laws that deprived blacks of their voting rights. These Jim Crow laws were supported by a series of decisions by the Supreme Court of the United States. The most influential case was *Plessy v. Ferguson* in 1896, in which the court supported the constitutionality of a Louisiana law requiring separate but equal facilities for whites and blacks in railroad cars. Eatonville, by being an all black town, was in the unique position of having no need to pass such a law, and was not affected by this blatant segregation.

Early Life in Eatonville

Six years after Eatonville's incorporation, it had between 200 to 300 residents—all black. Some men found year-round employment as citrus workers in the areas surounding Eatonville. Others worked as general construction laborers. Some worked on the railroad. Other men worked in Eatonville, itself, as house builders, shoemakers, cobblers, storekeepers. The women worked in vegetable gardens and groves, or as cooks and maids for the white residents of nearby towns.The children helped out with domestic chores, but all were strongly encouraged to attend school. With the founding of the Hungerford school in 1889, the children were able to receive an education within their own community, and were apt students.

In an advertisement in the *Seminole Print,* 1902, Vol. 2, 510, it was noted that the Fortnightly Club of Winter Park, Florida was featuring on its program, "Plantation Songs and Recitations by Pupils of the Negro Industrial School at Eatonville, near Winter Park to be held at the Seminole Hotel on Friday, Jan. 31, 7:30 pm and at the Sanford Hotel on Tuesday, Feb. 4, 7:30 pm. A Unique Entertainment! Don't Fail To Hear It!! FREE TO ALL!! All are invited to visit the School and see what is being DONE toward solving the Negro Problem." The advertisement ended with:

For dear the bondman holds his gifts
Of Music and of Song;
The gold that kindly Nature sifts
Among his sands of Wrong.
— Whittier

Another advertisement in the *Seminole Print,* 1902, Vol. 2, 563, announces that "Eatonville Makes Another Round in Her History. Mrs. Booker T. Washington, wife of the founder and principal of the Tuskegee Industrial School, will speak at the DEDICATION of BOOKER T. WASHINGTON HALL the New Dormitory, Tuesday, March 18, At 3 o'clock p.m. Every body invited to be present and hear the speaking."

St. Lawrence A.M.E. Church and Macedonia Missionary Baptist Church were the two early churches of Eatonville, and the mainstays of the religious and communal life of the town. Initially, both churches worshiped at the same location: St. Lawrence A.M.E. on the first and third Sundays and Macedonia Missionary Baptist on the second and fourth Sundays. In 1886, Macedonia acquired a separate dwelling on the corner of Eaton and West streets. All citizens were encouraged to attend one of the churches, and the children were expected to attend Sunday school. Most of the town officers, including the mayor, were active in either the Methodist or Baptist congregation.

Chapter 17

JOSEPH E. CLARK: A SUCCESS STORY

His success shows what colored men in the
south can do if they will.
Southern Industry 1907

As the fame of Eatonville grew, so did that of one of its founders, Joseph E. Clark. An article about Clark was published in *Southern Industry* 1907. It states that he is the principal merchant in Eatonville, and does considerable business in real estate. "He is one of the very first settlers of the town and has been largely instrumental in building it up to its present condition. He has lived in the town for eighteen years and has been in business since his first arrival."

It continues that "His stock consists of a well arranged stock of general merchandise" and recounts that J. E. Clark is Postmaster of Eatonville and also Chairman of the City Council, holding the office of Postmaster for sixteen years and City Council Member since 1895. "Few in his section have a larger farming business than he. His crop of onions this last season amounted to one hundred and fifty bushels, while all syrup sold in his store was raised on his farm. Six acres of melons have been planted and a car load was shipped on the tenth of June. He also owns two flourishing orange groves in the community. His prominent position among members of his race is shown by the office he holds as Treasurer of the Grand United Order of Odd Fellows for the State."

Another article attesting to Joseph E. Clark's fame was in an 1987 brochure, *Eatonville Centennial Celebration*, "Stories from the Past—J. E. Clark." It narrates that Clark was born in Covington, Georgia in 1859, and after the Civil War lived first in Chattanooga and then in Atlanta with his parents. He went to Florida as a teenager, working in orange groves for several years and saved his earnings and invested them in land as "opportunity offered." Clark became the owner of a considerable tract of land, and "it was upon his land that the Eatonville village and community were established. (Note: see Book III, Chapter 12.) Of course he has profited largely by this fortunate turn of affairs."

Joseph E.Clark served as mayor of Eatonville from 1899 to 1911—12 years.

The United States Census of June 18, 1900, Eatonville, Florida, indicates that Joseph E. Clark (age 40) was living with his second wife, Martha (age 47). The same Census also shows that Joseph E. Clark's younger brother, Isaac (age 33) was living in Eatonville with his wife, Laura (age 33) and their children: Beatrice (13), Oscar (10), Matilda (10), Joseph. (7) and Topbroina (3). The Census of 1920 shows two additional children: Theodore (8) and Catherine (6).

Joseph Clark's three daughters were now grown, married, and living in Georgia. He had a prosperous general mercantile business; was the owner of an orange grove of 25 acres, with more than 500 fruit-bearing trees; and the largest owner of real estate in the community (owning 25 houses and lots which he rented). By contrast, his brother Isaac was listed on the 1900 Census as a day laborer, and was not as successful as his older brother. He also had seven children. Joseph aided his brother and became a surrogate father to Isaac's family.

Much of what we know about Joseph Clark has been derived from the writings of Zora Neale Hurston, who was a writer, folklorist and anthropologist. She was raised in Eatonville and based many of her folklore tales on the people she observed in the town. Hurston mentioned Joe Clark(e) often, (adding the "e" to his surname). In her folk tales, she mentioned that she would "drag out leaving" Joe Clarke's store when sent there as a child, because she heard jokes, town gossip, and 'Bubber Mimms' blues Guitar."

Zora Neale Hurston was 46 when she wrote, *Their Eyes were Watching God.* Her character Starke was called Jody by his wife. In the *Eatonville Anthology* which she wrote in 1926, she shows Mrs. Clark calling Joe Clark "Jody." It is thought that the factual setting of Mayor Stark's funeral could possibly be what she saw of Joseph E. Clark's funeral, at which time she would have been about 19 years of age. At the age of 50, when Hurston wrote her autobiography, *Dust Tracks on the Road,* she had poignant memories of Mattie Clark(e) (Joe's oldest daughter) taking the pillow from under her dying mother's head.

Zora Neale Hurston was not popular with the townspeople of Eatonville because she portrayed them, thinly disguised, as caricatures in her folk stories using "literary license." Eatonville citizens were extremely proud of their town and their accomplishments, and felt her portrayals were demeaning, and that she never showed the pride and dignity of the people and the town. Zora, now has been vindicated because her fame kept the town alive until the townspeople's voices could be heard again.

Part of the description of Joseph E. Clark that Frank M. Otey mentioned in his book, *Eatonville, Florida, USA: A Brief History of One of America's First Freedmen's Towns* (FOUR-G Publishers, Inc. 1989), was that "Reportedly, he rarely smiled." The mean-spirited character of "Clarke" with an "e" does not equate with the real "Clark" without an "e" who helped establish, guide and supported a women's lodge, "Household of Ruth." (See Book III, Chapter 15.)

> *If I will it, it's no longer a dream . . .*
> unknown

Joseph E. Clark did realize his dream: to establish a "Black-owned, Black-run" town. Eatonville was officially established on August 15, 1887. In February, 1998, Eatonville was listed on the National Register of Historic Places as the first incorporated African-American municipality in the United States. It is the oldest black-owned, black-governed town in America.

Unfortunately, most of the town's original records were lost in a fire during the 1920s. After a town hall meeting, the clerk brought the town records home with him, as he often did. His house caught

67

fire that night, and the records were destroyed.

Joseph E. Clark, age 50, "Odd Fellow," died May 24, 1911, and was buried in the Eatonville Cemetery, Eatonville, Florida (fittingly in the town he founded and loved so much). Black Civil War Veterans were also buried in the Eatonville Cemetery.

With this telling of the saga of the Clark family and the extensive research that has gone into the writing of this "Labor of Love," it is hoped that:

> *There is nothing concealed that will not be disclosed, or hidden that will not be made known.*
> —Luke 12:2

In an article in the February 2001 issue of *O* magazine, Oprah was asked what her intention was when she made a movie of Toni Morrison's powerful novel *Beloved*. She answered: "My intention was to create a movie so powerful that it would allow people to feel, not just see, what it meant to overcome slavery and be able to love -- and to reconstruct a life." Our intention was for people to realize that this wasn't just a 'period' in history, that these were real people, our ancestors, who had fought their way back to some sense of humanity in ordinary and extraordinary ways. Oprah's words are extremely succinct. Insert "Book" for "Movie," and you have our motivation for writing this book. We are so very proud of our ancestors . . . what they overcame . . . what they accomplished.

It is our fervent hope and prayer that a Museum be established in Eatonville to commemorate and honor the Founding Fathers for their bravery and farsightedness.

The SAW MILL at Robert Hungerford Normal and Industrial School (circa 1940). Photo courtesy of Louise Franklin

Visiting Eatonville, December, 2001
(l-r) Calvin Mitchell, Louise Franklin, Olga Mitchell, & "Gus" Franklin
(Photo by Marion Civette Elden)

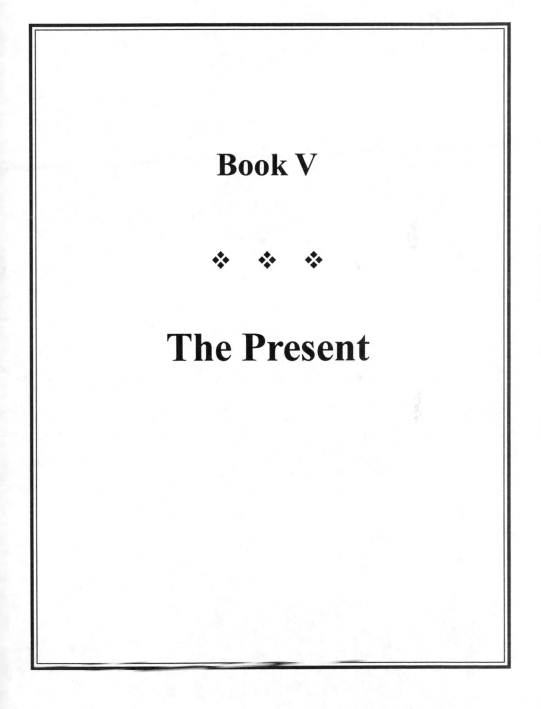

Book V

❖ ❖ ❖

The Present

Chapter 18

RECOLLECTIONS OF
Ms. Louise Franklin

Everything went on in Eatonville.
Everything was there for the Blacks.
Louise Franklin
Eatonville Elder and Historian

In researching this book, Olga Mitchell, great-granddaughter of Joseph E. Clark, founder of Eatonville, became acquainted with Louise Franklin, supporter and attendee of the St. Lawrence A.M.E. Church, when she visited the edifice for the first time. Olga was struck by Franklin's uncanny resemblance to her grandmother, Mattie. Both Louise and Mattie had the same coloring and high cheekbones. During their conversation, Louise said, "my father was a full-blooded Mohawk Indian." "My great-grandmother was a full-blooded Blackfoot Indian," Olga replied. Thus, began a bonding and an unique friendship.

Ms. Franklin is on the Eatonville Historical Preservation Board, and was always available to provide information and recollections of the town. She retained authentic records of the growth of Eatonville and very kindly shared them in the compilation of this book. "Mama told me to keep all records—they may be important in the future, she always said."

"Father, Larkin Franklin, was a full-blooded Mohawk Indian. He lived in Oklahoma and became a chauffeur. He did not take any foolishness from anybody. He would drive to Winter Park in the winter, and in the early 1900s, met my Mother, Effie Jackson, from Longwood, Florida (Mrs. Franklin lived to be 92 years old). Father married her and bought land on Lake Sybelia, Maitland, in the 1920s for $500 (expensive for that time) and owned the block (a block consisting of 10 acres)."

Maitland was being established now. In Zora Neale Hurston's autobiography, she wrote that blacks helped to build and lay out Maitland, and after a city election was held, Tony Taylor, a black man, became Unincorporated Maitland's first mayor; and Joseph Clark, another black man became Maitland's first town marshall. Workers were needed to work in town. Railroads were being built. Blacks came and settled around the lake in shanty homes. "These homes were too tight, and the blacks wanted to move out," said Louise Franklin. Joe Clark bought land next to Maitland, subdivided it, and sold it to any blacks that wished to settle there. "Why not a completely black town, run by blacks?" envisioned Taylor and Clark. Thus the town of Eatonville (two square miles) was on its way to becoming the first incorporated black town in the United States. Eatonville is still a tiny, picturesque town today with about 2,800 dwellers.

Augustus (Gus) Franklin, born on March 20, 1931 one-half block away from Eatonville provided the following lore: "The people of the towns of Maitland and Eatonville lived in harmony, whites and blacks, alike. The race riots of the 1920s in Ocoee never came to Eatonville. The white people of Maitland would protect the blacks and shelter them in their big homes. There has always been racial peace between predominately white Maitland and black Eatonville. It is one mile from the Post Office in Maitland to the main corner of Eatonville, and there has never been an instance of ill feeling between the two towns."

Ms. Franklin reminisced on early life in Eatonville. "We had Summer picnics. Mama made quilts, jellies and preserves and gave them away to neighbors. We had a nice time in Eatonville, everything went on there. Everything was there for the blacks. We all got along real nice. During Christmas, families would go and cut down trees and bring them back home to decorate. There would be a wonderful aroma. We would go visiting house-to-house."

Louise and her twin Lillian were born on July 28, 1936, and were only the second set of twins born in Eatonville. "It was a day to remember. All the old people were very excited that twins were born. School teachers asked permission to bring their classes to our home to see the twins. People would look at us and then at my Mother and ask, 'well, how did she do that?' Mama sewed for people in the community, and she was very humble, kind and good."

Although the Franklin family had acreage on Lake Sybelia and lived in Maitland, they always supported and attended St. Lawrence A.M.E. Church in Eatonville. Ms. Franklin attended St. Lawrence since

75

childhood and is still a very active and involved member. The children also went to school in Eatonville, attending the Robert Hungerford School.

In 1938, Louise Franklin saw George Washington Carver in person when he gave a speech at the school. Franklin has records from the Hungerford School addressed to her parents dated June 14, 1939: "My dear Sir: You are herewith informed that there is a small balance still due on your school account of $2.99." The Franklins also had (and still have) many friends in Eatonville.

During the early years of the community, and through the generosity of the Franklin family, community events were centered in a building on their property on Lake Sybelia in Maitland. This became a gathering place for baptisms, Boy and Girl Scout activities, social gatherings, and the men and women's lodge meetings. "Mama Effie had a license for blacks to come to the lake. She was very business-like and charged a small fee. In the summer, Boy and Girl Scouts from Orlando came and camped for two weeks at a time on our property on Lake Sybelia. During that time this was the only place where blacks could go for recreation. People from Orange, Seminole, and Osceola counties came for all holidays. There was nowhere else for blacks to go during that time. Many children would come after church to the lake and go swimming. My family had a wonderful life in Maitland/Eatonville."

After meeting Ms.Franklin on numerous occasions at St. Lawrence's Church, we were delighted to be given a tour of her property on Lake Sybelia. She told us that the property on Lake Sybelia is the only house in the community (still standing) that has a basement." There were only three original houses with basements at that time. My father was very wise. Everyone else had frame homes. We had the only brick house. People would come during storms and stay overnight in our basement."

In an article on Eatonville in *Florida Today,* Louise Franklin is lauded as the "town hall's goodwill ambassador." She smiles, makes phone calls and helps everyone. The love that she has for Eatonville/ Maitland is very obvious. She is indeed a Goodwill Ambassador.

Chapter 19

CLARK DESCENDENTS
EXPLORE THEIR HERITAGE

The Lot is fallen unto me in a fair ground:
yea, I have a goodly heritage.

Psalms 16:7

During the Summer of 2002, Olga Mitchell (great-granddaughter of Joseph E. Clark) had visitors from Canada: her daughter, Carol, and granddaughter, Erin . . . and the exploration of their heritage began with a visit to the town of Eatonville. Although they had heard many stories from Olga, and Grandma Dennis (Joseph Clark's daughter), about the town, Carol and Erin had never visited it. On a beautiful, sunny, cloudless August day in Florida, three generations of Clark descendents drove into the town of Eatonville. As they approached and entered it, Carol and Erin sighed with disbelief. This was actually the town that their direct ancestor, Joseph Clark, had founded, and in which Carol's beloved grandmother once lived.

Louise Franklin, Historian of Eatonville and its Goodwill Ambassador, was waiting for the group at the St. Lawrence A.M.E. Church. She was bubbling over with nostalgia about the town and the church and proudly showed them the beautifully and powerfully executed paintings mounted on the sanctuary walls of the church, and priceless original documents of Eatonville dating back to its inception. "My mother always told me to keep all records, and now I am glad that I did." These documents are now displayed at various historical locales by Franklin.

Carol grew very quiet as she literally pored over the papers with her daughter, Erin. When she looked up, she said, "I can't believe what I am seeing. To think that my beloved Grandmother Dennis used to worship with the congregation of this church; to think that she used to walk these streets; to think that I am seeing the area where she lived, it's so overwhelming."

Included in Franklin's papers were copies of the town newspaper, the *Eatonville Speaker.* Particularly interesting to Carol was an article on consumption, dated Saturday, June 22, 1889. "I have a positive remedy for the above disease, by its use thousands of cases of the worst kind and of long standing have been cured. So strong is my faith in its efficacy that I will send two bottles free, together with a valuable treatise on this disease to any sufferer. Give Express and P.O. address, T.W. Slocum, M. C., 181 Pearl St., NY." Carol was chuckling over this, because her Grandma Dennis always talked about consumption. "You will get the consumption, and it will kill you dead as a hammer," she would say. "Anything that could get you a cold—if your skirts are too short, or if you sit on a stone or something cold, you could get consumption."

Olga then stood up in church and delivered a moving soliloquy to the hushed audience about her family and what she discovered in her research (contained in this book). Clearly she was enjoying the experience of being able to impart this information to her daughter and granddaughter.

After leaving the church, the three generations walked around Eatonville. They observed a private home that is directly across the street from the present St Lawrence Church. This was the original 1881 church building. Of particular interest was the street in back of St. Lawrence Church that was named Clark Street in honor of the founder of Eatonville, Joseph Clark. Throughout the tour, Carol repeated: "But, this is where Grandma Dennis lived. I feel as if I'm walking where she did and reliving her stories about her childhood."

In 1997, Olga Mitchell providently happened upon a picture and article on Joseph E. Clark in the *Orlando Sentinel*. After intensive research, Mitchell validated that the Joe Clark in the picture was her great-grandfather. This was the final piece in the puzzle of the origin and roots of Olga Mitchell's heritage. Mitchell's most precious dream has finally been realized: the factual discovery of her heritage; and most importantly, the ability to share it with her beloved family!!!!

Pictures were taken of the three descendents—Olga, Carol and Erin—throughout the various locales of Eatonville as priceless mementoes of their visit.

Chapter 20

RETROSPECTION

A unique life is a work of art.
Eric Cassell

In Loving Memory of Grandmother Mattie Clark Dennis:

When you were telling us stories about your father Joseph Clark and what a "big" man he was, our young minds did not fully appreciate the enormity of what he had done in his lifetime. (All the more amazing for a black man.) Now, after researching material for this book, we can fully comprehend our direct ancestor's contribution to Black Society.

Thank you for the stories, Nannie. They weren't folklore. They were true. And we are so proud to be directly related to such a great man, to you, and to be descendents of the Clark Family.

Memories of Grandmother Dennis
by
Granddaughter Olga

"My Grandmother had the manners and bearings of a Lady"

My sister Gloria and I were so lucky to be raised and influenced by her, as both our parents, Bertha and Derrick Fenton, had to work.

Thinking of Nannie brings back memories of her loving and systematic ways. One morning she said to me, "It was so nice of that trolley driver to wait for me as I came down the street." She then proceeded to take off her hat and go about her routine. I was in a state of shock, because this was New York City where they would start the trolley with one of your feet still on the ground.

Meals were always waiting for us when we came home from school. She never raised her voice and expected us to obey her. It never occurred to us to be disobedient, and our parents would not tolerate our misbehaving.

Grandma had raised four girls, Lillian, Bertha, Bell and Maude in Atlanta, Georgia by herself after my grandfather, Will Pryor, did not return from a visit to Florida. Grandma could not read or write; therefore, the only link to her father was broken. Her oldest child was about 10 at that time. Grandma supported her girls by working as a domestic and in a restaurant. She walked 5 miles to the restaurant and 5 miles home; but the restaurant gave her the left-over food, and this was what she used to feed her family.

Maybe the genes of her Mother, Julia Hightower, who was a Blackfoot Indian, gave her the stamina. In spite of the adversities, grandmother somehow managed to see that all her girls attended school until at least the eighth grade.

In 1925, when I was born, my Mother asked Grandma to come North, stay with her and take care of me. A few years later my sister was born. Of course, Grandma stayed with us and enveloped us with her loving attentive ways.

Grandma always wore a hat and gloves with her outfits. Whenever we went to visit someone, we knew it was time to leave when Grandma would start adjusting her hat.

Going to church with Grandma each Sunday was a weekly trip to which I looked forward. She was well respected at her church, Mt. Moriah, in New York City. We always got there early, because Grandma always sat in the same pew each Sunday. Now, in retrospect, I would say she held court, because everyone would stop to visit.

I remember my Mother telling me that Grandma was going to 'Night School' because she refused to put an 'X' next to her name anymore. She did learn to write her name.

Grandma would always open her Bible and read out loud. But one day when I walked up behind her, I saw the book upside down. Mother explained that grandmother was talking through memory what she heard in church. My daughter Carol still has Grandma's Bible, and it is dogeared on the top and bottom.

Grandma then proceeded to care for my daughter Carol, as Carol's father and I had to work. Once, when she was caring for Carol, Grandma felt sick—as if she were going to pass out. She managed to call my sister Gloria, who in turn called me at work. I rushed from work, on the subway, scared and frightened because Carol was about seven months old, and no one else was there but Grandma. When I rushed in, Grandma had passed out, but she had placed Carol on the bed and threw her body over Carol's legs. Carol was just annoyed that she couldn't move. Grandma had a bad case of food poisoning.

Now that we know our family history, dating back to her upbringing in Florida and her father's vast orange groves, I can understand why Grandma insisted on an orange every day. Summer, Winter, Spring or Fall we had to always have oranges in the house.

When she died in 1976, Grandmother Dennis was around 100 years old. Grandma survived her four children. None of her girls, except my mother Bertha, had children. When our Mother died, our Aunt Doll insisted on taking grandmother back to Atlanta, Georgia. Aunt Doll's husband had died, and she lived alone in a lovely large house. A few years later, Aunt Doll died. My sister Gloria and I went down to Georgia and brought Grandma back to New York on her first airplane ride. She enjoyed it so much. My sister and I were apprehensive, as we hit turbulence, but Grandma was thrilled that she was being served food and ate everything off her plate. She was completely fascinated that they had a bathroom on the airplane. She really enjoyed that trip and always later enjoyed pointing to a plane and asking someone, 'Do you know what they do up there in that plane?'

Grandma's favorite saying, 'And This too Shall Pass,' contributed to her calmness.

About the Fentons . . .

In the 1940s, Father, Derrick G. Fenton, owned and operated a Medallion Taxicab in New York City. He was a knowledgeable gentleman, opinionated and prideful.

Mother, Bertha Pryor Fenton, worked a few years in a commercial laundry. In the 1950s she then became a "Homemaker" for the Children's Aid Society of New York, and was extremely proud of the fact that she was the first person to break the color barrier. "Homemakers" of the Children's Aid Society were assigned the momentous task of holding families together during crisis, and thereby, avoiding children having to be sent to an institution. She took great pride in teaching parental skills, how to handle the mechanics of maintaining a home, proper food shopping, and the like. Each case to her was an interesting challenge. Over the years, many appreciative families would send Mother Christmas cards with photos enclosed of her former clients.

About Olga . . .

Olga attended Howard University, Washington, D.C. She moved to Greenwood Lake, New York, after college and had a 43-year career, culminating in managerial positions, in the New York Telephone Company, NY (now known as Verizon); and Warwick Valley Telephone Company, Warwick, NY. She is now retired and living with her husband, Calvin Mitchell in Orlando (Hunter's Creek), Florida. Although from "Corporate America," Mitchell is a "Disney-aholic" and thoroughly enjoyed working at Disney's Polynesian Resort as a Disney Cruise Line Resort Representative for a number of years. She will always be proud that she was one of the "Opening Crew" when Disney Cruise Lines was established in July of 1998.

Daughter Carol attended the University of Prince Edward Island, P.E.I., Canada. She was vice president of the Student Union, and because of this position, received an invitation from the Lt. Gov. General of P.E.I. to attend Queen Elizabeth's Garden Party Commemoration of the Centennial Founding of Confederation. Carol was escorted by Brian; and they were married shortly thereafter.

Carol still resides in Canada with her husband, Brian and their two children, Jeffrey and Erin. The children are attending University in Canada, and Carol is employed in the Canadian School System.

Memories of Grandmother Dennis
by
Grandaughter Gloria

My memories of my Grandmother, Mattie Clark Dennis, will always be of happy times. She passed away at my home in 1976.

Footnote: In October of 2001, while I was working on this book, my doorbell rang. It was an Agent from the U.S. Department of Agriculture requesting permission to test for disease the lone orange tree I have growing in my backyard. I passed inspection and felt a surreal connection to my great-grandfather, Joseph Clark, and his orange groves.

When I was a young child, my Grandmother would come to our home to take care of my sister Olga and me while my mother Bertha was at work. She would fix my lunch and take me to school until I was able to go by myself. She would take me to the clinic when I was very sick. She would comfort my mother and me, and that meant a lot to us.

Nannie, as we would call her, would tell me the name of her father and mother—Joe Clark and Julia Hightower. She would say to me that her father was a "great man" and people would come from a lot of places to ask him to guide them in the right direction.

We now know that he founded Eatonville, Florida in 1887 and achieved a lot of important things in his life from age ten until adulthood.

My grandmother was a very religious person, and was an usher in her church. That was a good life for her and her second husband, Acy Dennis.

She always carried herself as a lady, because she was a person with a lot of class. I will always miss her because she was a kind and loving person.

About Gloria . . . .

Gloria married Wilbur (Bill) Magbie in New York City at the Convent Avenue Baptist Church, and was honored with a solo by Ms. McClain, her beloved choir director. The Church was Gloria's second home as a child and teenager, and she enjoyed singing in the Church

Choir, which was founded by Ms. McClain, a former operatic Broadway performer. She also joined the Girl Scouts at the Convent Avenue Baptist Church during the 1940s and later became a Girl Scout Leader.

After working at the New York Telephone Company, Magbie became a "Stay at Home" mom after the birth of her first child. She felt this enabled her to always be there to direct, comfort and guide her family. Her primary goal was to encourage her children to obtain a good education, and she is proud that she has been fortunate enough to see them accomplish these goals. The Magbie family consists of Gloria, husband Bill, children Linda and Paul, six grandchildren and one great-grandchild.

As the nest emptied, Gloria Magbie joined a women's bowling league; and building on her performing in the church choir at different venues around New York City in her teens, has taken courses in Dramatic Art at Nassau Community College. Now that Bill is retired, the Magbies travel around the country in their motor home, and have become officers of their travel club.

Mother Bertha and Grandmother Mattie have always meant a lot to Gloria, and when they became ill, she cared for them, and was with Mattie when she passed away. She appreciates the good childhood and upbringing she received from her parents and grandmother, and will always miss them.

Daughter Linda attended Nassau Community College, New York, and has worked in the medical field for over 20 years.

Son Paul, for many years, has been a member of Alpha Phi Alpha Fraternity, Inc. and Zeta Zeta Lambda Chapter of St. Albans, New York. In 2001, Paul also received a degree from Queens Borough Community College in Telecommunications Technology (Verizon), and in 2002 completed 28 years of service with Verizon.

Granddaughter Lisa received a degree from St. John's University and is planning a career in law. Grandson Robert attended college in New York City and works in a hospital there as a Pharmacist Assistant.

Grandmother was probably 102 years old when she died. An early Census shows her 10 years older than she acknowledged. Subtracting years from your age because of a need or vanity to seem younger was freely indulged in by many women during that time. Zora Neale Hurston subtracted 10 years from her age and confused her biographers for years.

Addendum: A New York Department of Health Certificate of Death, dated 6/25/76, 8:38 am, lists Mattie Dennis, Black, *92 years, of Nassau, Village of Hempstead. State of Birth, Georgia, U.S.A. Name of Father: Joseph Clark. Name of Mother: Julia Hightower. Dying of "Acute Cardiac Failure, Arterio Sclerotic Heart Disease."

Derrick G. Fenton and Bertha Pryor Fenton, holding their granddaughter, Carol, on her Christening Day in NY. (circa 1952)

About Bertha Pryor Fenton . . . .

A Certificate of Birth, Georgia Department of Public Health, Atlanta, Georgia, was issued to Bertha Mae Pryor, Negro, Female, on January 9, 1904. Place of Birth: Forsyth, Georgia. Father's Full Name: Will Pryor. Mother's Maiden Name: Mattie Clark.

Make the most of yourself, for that is all there is of you.
Ralph Waldo Emerson

IN LOVING MEMORY OF JOSEPH E. CLARK
—OUR PATRIARCH:

*   It's true that you only had girls.
*   Grandmother Dennis had just girls.
*   Our Mother had two girls.
*   Olga had a girl.
*   Gloria finally had a boy - and a girl.
*   You would have been proud of the accomplishments of your girls against all odds.
*   We are sorry that none of your direct descendents has carried the "Clark" name because we were all girls; but Great-grandfather, your genes are alive and well!!

Note:

As mentioned previously, our branch of the family only found our true roots in 1996.

Fortunately, Isaac Clark's family (Joseph's brother) carried on the Joseph Clark vision with great pride and dignity.

Isaac's family has commanded great respect in their personal dealings and accomplishments.

We would particulary like to THANK the dynamic Bobbye Alexander and her spouse, Hubert Alexander (his mother, Catherine Clark Alexander was Isaac Clark's daughter) for the warm, enveloping welcome of our branch into the family fold.

Olga Fenton Mitchell
Gloria Fenton Magbie

REFERENCES

Archival Sources:
American Historical Society, Inc., NY
Eatonville Historical Preservation Board, Eatonville, Florida
Maitland Historical Society and Museums, Maitland, Florida
Orange County Regional History Center of Central Florida
Orlando Public Library of Orange County Florida
Rollins College Archives, Winter Park, Florida
U.S. Dept. of the Interior, National Park Service
U.S. History Society, Inc.
U.S. Post Office Archives
White House Historical Association

Book I - Chapters 1, 2, 3

Census Sheets, 1860, OPL
*Compton's Interactive Encyclopedia Deluxe,*1997,The Learning Co., Inc.
http://www.historychannel.com/perl/world_timeline.pl?year=1850
Orlando Sentinel, page 8, 10/9/77, OCRHC
Pictorial Encyclopedia of American History, 1861-1865, USHS
The Presidents of the United States of America, 1995, WHHA
*The World Book Multimedia Encyclopedia,*1998, *World Book Inc.*

Book II - Chapters 4, 5, 6, 7, 8

Associated Press
Census Sheets, 1870, OPL
*Compton's Interactive Encyclopedia Deluxe,*1997, The Learning Co., Inc.
Hamer, Philip M., Ph.D., *Tennessee, A History, 1673-1932,* AHS, 1933
Reece, Colleen L. & Donihue, Anita Corrine, 1984, *Apples for a Teacher*
The Last Two Million Years - Reader's Digest, 1974
The World Book Multimedia Encyclopedia, 1998 World Book, Inc.
USA Today

Book III - Chapters 9, 10

Census Sheets,1870, 1880, OPL
Georgia, OPL
Hanna, Dr. A. J., 1986, RCA
James, Marjory, *Eatonville: A Story of Negro Management,* 1986, RCA
Stark, Peter, *The Old North Trail, Smithsonian Magazine,* 1998

Chapters 11, 12, 13

Andrews, Mark, *Flashback,* the *Orlando Sentinel,* October 20, 1991, August 15,
    1999, RCA
Andrews, Mark and Robison, Jim, *Flashback,* the *Orlando Sentinel*
Eatonville Speaker, 1889
Logan, Irene, Historian, MHS
New York Sun, 1891
Otey, Frank M., *Eatonville, Florida, A Brief History,* 1989
USPO

Chapters 14, 15

Franklin, Louise, *A Call To Worship,* 2003
Curtis, William C. H., Worthy Grand Scribe, *Ritual of the Household of Ruth,*
Grand United Order of Odd Fellows, 1962, Eighth Reprint of 1911 Edition
Franklin, Louise M., Maitland, Florida, Historian, EHPB
    Note: Ms. Franklin provided the original books for review on the Lodges:
    books dated - August 1883, Richmond, VA, and August 1887, Nashville, TN
National Register of Historic Places, Continuation Sheet - Section 8, Pages 6, 7,
    USDI, OCRHC
Saint Lawrence AME Church Brochure, 2001

Book IV - Chapters 16, 17

Census Sheets, 1900, OPL
Eatonville Centennial Celebration, "Stories from the Past - J. E. Clark," 1987
Florida Living, February 1998
Knight, Anthony B. Jr., Curator, *Town of Eatonville, Prospectus,* 1997
Logan, Irene, Historian, MHS, from Research at University of Central Florida
Nat'l Register of Historic Places, Eatonville, Historic District, Orange County, FL,
    USDI
O, February 2001

References

Seminole Print, 1902, Vols. 2, 510 and 2, 563, RCA
Southern Industry, 1907, OCRHC

Book V - Chapter 18

Ebony, 1946
Florida Today, 1987
Franklin, Louise, Historian, EHPB

About the Authors

Olga Fenton Mitchell

After attending Howard University, in Washington, D.C., Olga Mitchell moved to Greenwood Lake, New York and had a 43-year career with the New York Telephone Company and the Warwick Valley Telephone Company, Warwick, NY, as Manager of the Tariff and Training Departments. Upon her retirement, Olga and her husband, Calvin Mitchell, moved to Orlando, Florida, where she worked at Disney's Polynesian Resort as a Disney Cruise Line Representative for a number of years. She has also worked at the Cornell Fine Arts Museum, Rollins College, Winter Park, Florida, as a docent (informational exhibition guide) for the Cosimo Rosselli exhibition. Rosselli was a Renaissance artist and a painter of the Sistine Chapel, the Vatican.

Mitchell's daughter, Carol, lives in Canada with her husband Brian and two children, Jeffrey and Erin.

Gloria Fenton Magbie

After working at the NY Telephone Company, Gloria Magbie became a "stay-at-home" mom following the birth of her first child. She felt this enabled her to always be there to direct, comfort, and guide her family. As the nest emptied, she returned to some of her earlier pursuits, including taking courses in Dramatic Arts at Nassau Community College.

Now that husband Bill is retired, the Magbies continue to travel around the country in their motor home. At one time they both served as vice president and president of their travel club.

About the Authors

Marion Civette Elden

Marion Civette Elden was born in Newark, New Jersey, and subsequently moved to Billerica, Massachusetts with her daughters, Donna, Lisa, Michele, and Suzanne. She worked in advertising and public relations; as a journalist, typesetter and copywriter for a local newspaper; and as a graphic arts/computer teacher, graduating Magna cum Laude from Fitchburg State College, in Massachusetts. Elden also attained a M.Ed. from the University of Massachusetts and was inducted into the international teaching honor society, Phi Lambda Theta.

Marion and her husband, Ray (also a teacher) are now retired and live in Hunter's Creek in Orlando, Florida. They are substitute teachers in the Orange County School System, and she is an editor and journalist for the magazine *Life in Hunter's Creek*. The Eldens have a combined total of 10 children and 25 grandchildren.